Transient – A Temporary Abode

Amitav Chakraborty

PARTRIDGE

ISBN: Softcover 978-1-5437-0844-8
eBook 978-1-5437-0845-5

Print information available on the last page.

To order additional copies of this book, contact
Partridge India
000 800 919 0634 (Call Free)
+91 000 80091 90634 (Outside India)
orders.india@partridgepublishing.com

www.partridgepublishing.com/india

Contents

To Begin With ...

Few experiences written as notes...
Here, I participate,
In your thoughts !!!
While in your warmest hands...
Kept away, for so long.

Destined but to be with you,
While you kept always in your eyes,
Lest I do fumble,
Each words, are consigned to you.
The one, that has made me and the one, that I shall be is only by you.

Read them, as I felt for only the goodness,
Of the intent to partake...
The little experiences that I gathered as a tiniest possible dot...
Now in your hands is my creation of words
This is one step more
To be with your wise conscience
To learn more and hear even more
To be placed in the book shelf of your
rooms

So divine yet so naive ...
Please bless me with your eyes and ears
The notes 're not anything out of This world.
They were taught to me by the power of Lord.
Now that I lay in your most adorned hands.
Bless me more ...
Bless me more ...

Transient

Oops for the dying beauty,
Oh the enchantment of desires !
If the home given is so transient
What is the hurry of not being there...
Why so fast, you think and act...?
Is that you are afraid of the enact?
Look for the creations so monumental ...
The length of the rivers and the impasses.
What does the mountains reflect ...

Are they even bothered for the huge air that deflect ?
Wealth... wealth and more so wealth,
Put a stoppage somewhere !
The ephemeral sorroundings around you...
Measure sometime, how pure or impure.
The transient never stays, you also have to learn,
To stop and gaze !!!

Having A Mind Of Our Own

I am the best friend, of my own,
And Its good that, I have a mind of my own !
The heart has you in it ...
And that's how sweet it is.
No one woul d live without you,
Whither shall I go, from thy spirit !!!
The beats of my heart and the stars I gaze in the night has all of you...
Guide me my god to blend my heart and mind to one soul
Then can I live a little strong...
Then can be freed from some of the fears,
Flowers () preach to us ... I am trying to hear.

What is in the silence of the sky and the bodies that it bears !
Each road I want them to be a fragrant shrine,
Why I don't bow, when I see the forms they made you exist,

Why I go blank in the temple and the mosque
You are me and I am you!
Chivalrous just to me to usher you more...
More of mine I had its just time for you to reign !

With all possible ardour, I want to just reveal,
How much I now owe,
For giving me a mind of my own.
With the gestures that may not be shown,
Let me move ahead with the shape of you in that.

Eternal bliss

I am in a mansion the beach is besides...
But when the sun sets it darkly so ceases !
What is the use of the marbles that I brought
Bring me some sunshine come and embrace even if in my longing thots !
Only then I can see the waves ....

Your presence is the only due,
Rest all seems fulfilled now,
The farmers in their lands waiting for the plough
Where is the pair of sparrow, flown.
For the full moon to bring a mere charity,
I need you to make this a reality.
Whatever comes and go, feels no sorrow,
With you the life would be a vibrant flow.
Without you everything will be a miss,
Like the archer aiming for the gold,
Stood now reminiscing and old, for the one inch of foul.
Oh the elernel bliss of mine,
Do not take more so time,

Make it a triumphant moment for me,
Take the fastest of the mode now to come,
Least few more moments are lost ...
Sit inside me in my heavens, it’s so lost.

Butterfly Kiss

I'm still alive and I don't know why?
My heart survived falling from the butterfly sky.
Caught by the hands of destiny.
With visions only I can see!
My love I heard your call.
Wings of a butterfly broke my fall.
Love motion is in the air, a love no one can compare.
Indulging a look-a stare~that we both share.
Reminiscing our love made out of steel.
Awe~:*! To them butterfly kisses that felt so real!

Flowing like Amazing Grace,
a shining light upon my face.

I traveled fast and far, longing to be in your arms.
I desire the warm sensation of your charms.
Your safe love will help me carry on,
with the strength and bond~the love you set upon.
Nothing is better than a sensual butterfly kiss.
Beyond the sensation of heaven's pure bliss.
Fluttering in the clouds aiming for the moon.
A dream of reality, out of my cocoon I bloom!
Valued by the art of true beauty and it's rarity.
True love flapping in the mist of clarity.
I entwine that I am yours and you are mine.
Bonded together till the end of time.
With the vision my heart is no longer blind.
Two broken heart at last combined.

Indoctrinate Me

Your absence is your presence,
Distances are so inspiring...
These words are your gift !
To treasure my times so missed.

I cannot escape the web
Woven around you ...
By the mystique nature,
That looks upto and it finds you.

Thankfully one more day tossed out,
To bridge the place there where you are
Promise you me stood all tall,
Finding the feet to fall.

Ubiquitous

With your presence so far yet you are everywhere,
In All of my redemptive times and the severe ones you are there.

You look at me and I in in you !
Yet, some times, I forget that you repose here in me.

Some act of mine which I do and for a moment I forget,
I do all those only to be with you.
Each day and each moment of time I step near you...
I cannot do any wrong, I cannot see any wrong...just

Make sure that you hold me in your hands
So blissful...
That all I forget and come nearer so nearer to you !!!

7 Sisters

God from above do you see,
We are cut from the rest...
With a narrow strectch,
just below the lofty mountains.
The frozen ice, melting into fluid.
Our blood has steamed a lot,
The venial acts of few do not bother much...
The delayed so justice
We are so resilient ...
The land bear these leaf which we call the T,
The bird, has a yellow beak, which even puts the goldsmith baffled,
The limestones has no comparison !
The dance with few bamboo sticks,
Even God Krishna found his own,
The magic found in a gemstone

All From North East (Let's Poise This Imbalance)

U r unbalanced
That's why u r asom
U r love
That's why u r so far
U have the rivers and the hills
That's why u mesmerise me and all
You are my land with fruits so fine
I want to dine under the pine
No it's not the dream given by wine
It's your smell when rains, it's you when I think of you.

Is It The Rain That I Cry

I can cry this rain for you
Missing every station and moments as you grow each day
If only the Train stops here now and forever
I would love you and your mom to be my only co - passenger
To take you to the drive where angels only will greet you !
To make the only presence of you in the time and days to come
Everything should be won over and lost at your innocence
The storm within me will calm down
Just waiting and looking at the sun going down
Knowing that some day it rise with your only presence.
Now that you have grown and utter soft words
When I am with you now all my pain seems gone.
For a perfect day has come the moon and the sun have come both
One asking the other, to bless the father
What ever happens now shall be more merrier ...
The wait so long has borne the fruit,
Of being ever so more happier !!!

Where Do I Belong !

Where do I belong, I belong to nowhere.

Silently each day I rise but with you
Born to be a refugee in this arms of river and green trees
Of people who came before me and named me such
Now I love not more in you since the peace has broken
The innocence has been taken away...

But not by you,
That is when I try to reach back again,
In the broken sheets of those glass panes.
To gather them one by one ...
Even if some blood sheds,
Even if some die to born again,
Since you are there to be my friend again
Why would that name be mine
I can only be a refugee in you and no one else
You never would say no to anyone saint or a deadly sin

The crops that they sowed and became green by the hard work even on the sunny days
Made your place green

Why you allow them to run at night when they should be curled up and wait for the morning sun
But they rose to the sound of killing wild fire only to burn their thathced hamlets
Spreading hands to hold some infants and some toddler who cant even walk
Who was there with them when the fear of death so overcoming was there looming in
The deadly nights and the narrow village alley
Holding on just to few broken stems of the tree
Breathing just not to be heard of, or the machete and daggers
Would just rip them for the last
Sounding not even when the most lovely possessions were felled
Holding just on to you and breathing for the last some survived
To the power of love that you spread
To try and to try again to forget
Ghastly nights and the deadly hands
You made me what I am now, take away the name given by them
Take away the hatred even with you I possess
And allow me to live a life unsoiled
Allow me to write my experiences for all new ones to come
Overpower me now since you are "borderless"
Come to the rescue at any moment when the tragedy strikes
No religion no devil no imprudent can touch all

Come out now from the temples, mosque those in some corners of this villages
And sow the fields with them hand in hand
Make them bloom again make them never wilt by the man who came before me.

Can the borders of countries can be written by the rivers or mountains
Or is it that to survive then to live is more salient
Make this world "borderless"
That's how I surrender to you, that's how I named my lines as such
Rain the love rain the courage and remain like that my love.

The Desires To Be With You

Oh the smooth wind and the thought of the sea ...
Whenever there is this rush,
Rush... of want to be with you !
Started this rush, when my eyes opened though I missed you whole the previous day,
Look, its past noon, and I am still much left with the desire to be with you

With your eyes smiling into me,
With your small arms, trying to reach out,
The kind of speed, you want to show,
I just want you slow that grow...
For, I want to stay a bit young and mad,
I want me to make small things of joy for you
I am learning how to play the instruments ...
Those who make the heart melt !
Will you give me sometime my little angel ?
To make my world rich with love, that never was there in me,

Each moment when you overturn the pages of your life then,
You can dance your beautiful steps...

Be gracious enough, to be tender, yet so resilient,
This austerity of life will just smile away,
One more day, I want to hold you when we walk in this ...
Lawns of life, this shall have the roses and the spikes,
How I make you to choose either and

The Child Is Running Away

So many times I passed by this shop
So many times he served me those hot cup of sauce
I looked at him and I felt
The child in him is running away from him

I expect him to hold those glasses lean into my hieght
And say, sir here is the order you place
Comeon now what do I expect
My own angel in an air condtined school
And you are here to serve those glasses
Of milk and the juices so cool.
You don't have to answer like a adult
You just need to hold on that age
Come on my friends let not make this child run away.

You bring Joy
You bring joy to the place you live
And the place you live is warmth and soft
It is our heart that you are there ...
And it shall never stop beating with joy

Wish you a happy 2 nd birthday with doubts of whether it is nice
That you grow or you be a small little baby doll like you are now when you are 2 years young.

Keep your mind as fresh and new
Keep creating new things and those magic with your smile
Take blessings from all special people
Who have enriched and showered their love
By just being there !

With all the times that made us more strong in the past
With your presence we feel more and more just
You have healed us and have not taken any fee
That makes me believe more and more
Things that bring joy are gifted by God and they are free !

Building a castle of strength to up-bring you
I promise of not imposing anything on you
But to help show you the world and make you choose
Let us begin this humble journey now without getting late !
This universe has enough good - ness to be taken from

Small caring tread with your tiny feet now, let us help you make them understand.

Listening To Learn

Too much of a crowd everywhere ...
Each step might fall on a trap.
Be wise by listening to all,
View even the bottom ones... not only the tall.

The seasons of spring and fall,
Like the sun and the moon,
Like sometimes dark even in noon !
Give ear to the seasons bloom, much around...

Amongst the darkest night...
Millions of sparkling stars shine,
They are also for you,
Not only for those who think they are the divine.

For god may even ask you,
Without any bias I stood !
Why then my own self you sometime fear,
Also how can you feel some are more dear.

At me the world begins and ends,
At me the powerful and the tiniest dwell...

You are very much a part of the whole,
Let no one ever thus dig a hole.

Carry on with the torch of light,
That will illuminate both the wrong or the right.
The present confusion that you have,
Will definitely see the ray of broad day light.

Your ears, will be filled some day,
Suddenly with a voice so nice,
You shall arise from the sleep of reprise!
That is the end to begin again, that is the idea of sounds
that ask you to listen.

My Earlier Shape

Do not ask me my earlier shape
Time has taken away those michivoius days
Even if I want to bring them back
They keep asking me to look only ahead.

Why did then I lost so much in the past
Was it to gain my lost love
Way much fast ?
Oh yes, now I made up the lost days.
Why still I go back to those days..
Where the stream flew with no noise
The curves of the roads though rough were
Travelled through with a wish of meeting again.
No wealth not even the hope for that
There was a love that use to call
There was no intention of any one to expect.

Call Of The Next Day

Oh all my destined child,
Don't be wild ...don't be wild !
This is an unheard call from a distance,
For all, to wait for the call of the next day.

The wheels of time was stoppable by none,
Give a pause, do not try even to cry !!
Or you will loose, some precious drops of pearls
Keep them inside you, why don't you just try.

The distance call is neutral for all,
Catch them right when you are standing alone.
For those cannot be heard when the crowd gathers,
You my not be able to choose from worst or the better.

You have a brilliancy of your own
With that just keep moving on.
No matter if it rains or the sun is at the glare most,
Open the umbrella of faith inside the unseen world of your own.

Coz life is interwined not by you but by me living far way so far...

Your thoughts and imagination only can reach up there
Yes, but in the solitude that you spent
You will find the briefest possible rest...
Your pact is hence to carry on
Forgetting even the very closed bastion
No matter who kept you warm all through till now
It might happen that you are made one now
But the breathe that you take and the eyes that winks
Shows very much something inside you is still not that weak.
Today is already heard now with the facts most possible...
Wait for the call of the next day be a little gentle.
For the fear of the unknown might be there, but many of you still be facing the white glow.
The glow shall come only after it I set and I rise ...
Wait for the call of the next day ... it of course also shall be pleasant surprise.

After Your Hands, The Eyes And Then In Your Thoughts

When you now picked this up to read,
Just before remitting in the book shelves
Let me soak in the eyes and
Try to settle in a small space of your mind.

Let me learn from my mistakes
Let me gather in few more words
To make me write only for you.
The life lead so far will be a conquest.

Only if you allow me that way
Of not just being in the hands ...
Soaking away whatever pain or the sorrow you have.
A gentle flow of breeze shall I try,
To be in your mind when you

Back Stage Conversations

I am in the open field to play the game
I am not here to hear some backstage conversations and to blame
It was there and it shall ever continue
With some trying to judge and put few names
I am here to play my own learned game.
The coaches are you here to give me the learnings
The bad few still keep observing...
Trying to act a path for me after the backstage converstions
That I fail to hear see.
I am now in this open field to play my game.
Not the two posts and that net ...
There are so many of them,
Each play I shall now overcome,
The back stage talks have made me that strong !
I have a strange feeling of an emperor ...
That today the game that I play.
Shall be rewinded again and again
The play that I am planning now, has come far ...
Judge don't me by the talks of the corridoors ...

Watch me play my own expertise.
For I am not here to blame ...
I shall from here play my own made games.
My friends I have not withdrawn, I feel this way ... the game is on.

Picnic Times

Every year round this time,
I have my friends and I have my dear one's ...
Always, I am filled with positive vibes,
The flock of birds flying high.

The start in the morning so fine,
With my dad and Mom I feel divine.
The forest so kind with green trees in line...
I see a blue vast clear sky,
Which I miss seeing from my home midst the polluted air.
The Joy of being together, has no bounds,
The time is passing very fast now.
The picnic times are a treasure for me, when I grow ...
Keeping them as a memoir for me to show.

A Little Beyond Oneself

Comrades in arms or without it even
The winning point was always looking beyond oneself
Hand in hand we were trained
To defend the glory of the motherland.
We climbed, we swam ...
Looking back it was impossible without the arms of
All of us little beyond oneself.
The bullets were not written for us
We survived the coldest dust
We ran for covers within ourselves
A team made us win that.
Flock around comrades not alone.
The signs of footsteps shows that you are herd so strong.
That's the only things the enemy will follow
And the loved young one's will emulate.

The Quite Moon

Learned from the moon to be alone
Quietly amongst the burning blooms
Of so many stars and the uncolored azure.
Sits quietly with different shapes,
Passing each time as a panoramic view,
From the plain earth a few.
Took to the roof of the house,
Quietly though it gave ...
Enormous amount of free bountys
Hey the way you move
How can you be so ageless and so without sound
What is it that you show
How is that you keep the go...

Slow and slow.
The lost vestiges do not show you moved
I am living far from some of my closest moor
Still they say you are equally visible.
How is the reticence so loud ?
Drops of water frosted so
Showing the signs of time for you to go,
The usurp one shall come soon.
The fluttering flocks and the moving beasts
How long would the wait to be seen
Breaking the shackles not to be burnt
Urging you most soon to be come.
Oh, the wait in the sun !
Where Is the moon so quite now gone.

Long Journey

Twigs of broken trees, some standing very tall
Swept by the nights rain
Gathered on the road with shining sand.
No speech no motion
Unfurling each meanders
Tides reaching out even on surface after that huge crush !!!
Bounded by few in some length of the odyssey
Yet so much curves and
And more curves unexplored!
The journey begun so is only half done,
With more joys and sorrows it shall sure come.
The fallen leaves and twigs, shall each unfurl,
Into the success and also the failures that shall follow.
The long journey named 'life' in itself,
Has amazing strength and happiness, may be its inside a shell.

Songs Of My Solitude

Drops of melting sky
In the vast pastures deep inside me
Wants to bloom into a twigs of cherry blossom
The hymns and the sounds of silence is gaining a little momentum,
There is lot of noise outside,
Make me see and hear my own insight,
The songs of my solitude, is the treasure kept me so tight.
The warmth given to deflect the so cold winter.

Where Is The Time To Write

Every moment I am short of time,
Only running, to fulfill desirous so yield.
The depot even if it is full,
My innate desire is make some

Where Is The Perch Of Inspiration?

Longing the arms of soft caress
Wanting a shade to sit
Where do I find a perch that does not allow any kind of breach
So that I feel, I act
And I some kind of music to create.
Oh the noisy world be it far or near !
Do not make it so crammed,
Give everyone time taken bit to act...
Do not leave the home turf unprepared
There are demons to swallow each step of you.
As you feel from your own instincts ...
Yet few you can always reach !
Even be careful of the circumstances ...
The tyranny of time would have left them,
Finding a perch of inspiration
Wanting a shade to sit ...
The search has grown more longer than ever before
Quite a very few left to shoulder on.

The Path To Follow

Wake up my sons and daughters..
Wake up for the one time to bridge
Even if the energy is so forceful of the waters
The chosen bricks
By the very hands of you the braves...
The crafter that I know you as,
Shall overcome all the thirsty craves.
The way that shall be made only by your careful steps
Each day that you thought and act
Look...look now how at the core you stand.
Gentle air of blessings
Everywhere so unseen
Catch them only for you they mean...
Keep move of a potent flow.
Nothing extraordinary is achieved by a thought
Every day your legs must run for some more
Resting at times when needed,
Wake up for the one more time to bridge
Even now if the rivers have reached the shore
And there stands a vast body of basins,

You have known and learnt the art by now
Building a bridge as never before.
The bow of the rain, so distant
And the desire to

The Barman Is Listening

Open the windows and doors
Even in closed closets with so many bottles
If you speak a word the barman listens to the world.
That previous day when some died
With a medicine imbibed
The turn on that road ...
Made by somebody so broad
In the brink of that sweet wine
The medico and the driver opined.
That no more now remained a secret,
Everyone now wanted a few more describes.
Oh the gravest secret of the newly wedded bride,
How come it came up in a broad day light.
The money so hidden deep deep inside
By the so powerful and the might.
The next turn of the day,
When planned to make the hey,
The enemies have the secret now !
The glass of wine made me opine
Called by the ministry higher ups,
Reprimanded for the unknown lapses.

Under the lenses
Now he stands ... the night before in the ears of no one
But the barman on the stand.
The uniformed guard tired and retired
Favored some and some bulldozed.
After him were few friends and a few foes,
With a glass of wine he vowed..
The barman though closed his eyes ...
His ears were forced to pierce,
Oh the wiser lot,
If ever you happen to forgot,
The actions of yours are being monitored,
Very few are left free scot.
You being in the not so lucky lot,
How would you account which barman
Did left loose your notes.
So many of them are on the road.

Honesty Killed In Different Ways

The newspapers bears the aftermath of the days
Honesty it seems killed again and again.
The very foundations of the globe...
Now reins in the hands of a few grown,
Bigger than they thought they would,
Now they have to protect all the moulds.
No looking back now as if the chapters are closed now,
How many innocent lives killed by the collateral blows.
No one to even contemplate ...
Weakened are fearful,
And the learned knew the Law,
How much to be paid to whom, now is since few are in the claw.

The signs of the deeds are visible by some bodies that do not any further move,
If only God comes and tells us the truth,
For the judge himself now will be in a prove,
The commitment is known both to the evil and the death.
The nations grew by each hands of the peasants,

Why then individually there is no attendance,
Where would they go...
Where would they show ...
The burnt skins underneath the softly woven threads that bear the attire,
The lashes that were given by the rich opulent,
Alone they bear it not on days but years.
The changes happened not by the stroke sudden,
Few policies and amendments ...
Took the way of being official,
Peeped through the window and found the same giants.
Now if the honesty to be proven,
Why and when can it be shown to the unknown ?
Why is that the good things, my lord, takes time for the beaten,
What is the path ahead for the good man,
Are you asking him to be all alone ?
Why your calls are subdued,
Why the giants have those attitude ...
They keep moving with the jeweled car,
Why would the honest left with the scar,
Asked you so, as I know,
There may still be a pebble, I would like to throw,
In the sludgy waters to come and show,
Where does it goes and strikes,
Able to fend me a solace of thoughts,
Raise ....Raise ... the honest to keep the flow.

My Benchmate

My benchmate is a happy freak
He and she knows each day to be happy and dance
For their fathers knows the trick,
They are the seeker in the high scrappers,
Built on the land of those penniless.
I was equally reciprocating,
Till the time the opportune came,
I who strolled night and day,
Stood failed, but they hailed ...
Yes, they acclaimed...
Yet then though I struggled ...
I kept moving with my own beaten soul,
Lifting every fallen leaves on the way, which were given by the day.
The frosty nights did not ditter,
The pale foggy path even were fought.
Now that I have learnt the tricks ...
I have equal chances for a retreat.
Bring the drums, bring the mike
Its but better to bring a page to write.
To keep the notes for ages to come,
These were the gifts of the wise sages of time,

Knowing no one in mind did they wrote...
My bench-mate we meet seldom so,
They wear the silky vests,
And I wore mine made with timeless scale.

Far Above In A Plane Of Hope

Breaking the shackles of my daily life
Want to see how the earth looks like,
The ones that give so much pain,
Are they visible even,
When I take off with the heights in the plane.

Let it take me up up and up
Flying above the white solidified ...
Above when I see it would be the pure sky,
Below would be a roundish, dot.
Can I make my horizon so broad ...
Visibly enough can I draw a few straw.

With a point of conjencture,
Where the day seeks permission to end up the play,
The night is worried to narrow someone down,
Flying high above the ground.
Wearing a plain white sheet,
Reflecting the rays of whatever falling on it.

Now the plane will take turn,
The majestic views of your actions,
Shall now be shown,
You have done so much,
The toughness of you the breathing soul,
Look look them now in whole.

Want To March Forever Now

When now there is no life
And no one to even see that few cry
Or the luaghters that I made
Sitting nested in the group of old friends.

If the walk is so easy now,
When there are no roads nor the signs,
I am marching above the clouds,
With the neighbours not so loud.

Slippery they are but not that conflict...
Faced when I was part of the earth,
Beautiful stars make the party more so nice,
In the jar of blissful bellows.
That I walk alone does not make any interference,
The view I hold of all is what the difference...
The good creatures of God,
Everyday they come out to trod.

The time spent more or less,
With relatives and the friends in hoards.
Some days passed

Travelling To Your Country

Bought a ticket ever so dear
Travelling from the dearest country to all that is yours !!!
Will you embrace me with all then and not let me fall,
Your country is as dear as mine, I am told.
With a speech that may be different ...
With a skin which my be a little not fair,
Will you embrace my sons and daughters,
Who are so well by me admired,
Will you not let the press to write anything not pleasant so...
I shall wait for them to come back at times
Back to me with the culture that you sow ...
What would be more better than to see,
Countries giving blended knowledge to all,
Forgetting the walled barriers, here my sons and daughters
Trying to fly away to the western shores.

The Towel Of Life Has Lots Of Moisture

The passing sun, would you be able to dry
The kept towel, outside the house,
Its kept hanging by the two limbs of mine,
It has captured a lot of moisture
Of days gone by.
Most of them were soaked in from the outside vibes,
All of them could have been avoided ...
Though I understand late in times.
Some of them came from dearest sweethearts,
Unknowing though, they came unplanned.
Between the sweetness and the sour,

I am always choosing the shout of the far,
To be with me sweetest one's...
Leave some of them my loving sun.

The House Chimney

Am I there to lift up the smoke inside
What would I do when the clouds ...
Come in flocks and cover all outside.
Yes, as I can see...
Beyond the wavering pine trees,
Few brunette, gather.
They have an intention of a storm,
Building like never seen,
The fliers have also caught them in their radars,
The folk on the ground kept informed.
Am I here to only look and feel,
Give me a means and some ways, to some, I want to reveal.
For remaining on the highest mount of the house,
I cannot avoid looking around...
Enough of vanquished smoky puffs have I swollen,
While going up, they try to waver and solace...
The burnt and dead woods that they are produced,
Waiting for the earth to shake, my owners then ...
Might send the masion to heel few bends,
I shall catch them by the hands,
If only then I can make them turn and show the,
Plans of the black eyed heaps !
Keep the barrel and stocks ready before they rain.

The Arrow That Guides

Never mistake an arrow that guides
If you do so, it will have the time lost and imbibed.
You have to offroad if need be,
Fast coming back to track !
Spend very less of time in listening to your self.

The want of a Child
Read that purest smile, curved like a days aged of the new moon...
The

The Elephant Rider

You are so giant yourself, the eyes are stuck at you,
The rider though has the tiny stick that guides you.
Not a single passerby that I see ...
Who is not amazed by the alluring way you move ?
The rider has the key, the footmarks but are borne by you.

The Desire To Success

Failing enough, I have a desire to succeed now,
Let me see the sound of success, enough of silence deafened me till this time.
The dark engulfing evening and the nights,
Let me get up with a bearing light.
Come and face me on the curve,
Stoic that I am, with a time inhaled.
What have the time taken from me is not as important,
The versatility I have attained.

Scaffold

Look he may just be moved
With a face not to be seen,
Waiting gaurds, lower the sheen,
One more death, makes no difference.

Be A Pragmatist

Nothing is achieved beyond a limit,
Apply the basics,
Time they say is less, if not much !
Even then, being a pragmatist helps.

The path on the way to the garden of fruits,
There is a laden tree, almost heavily bearing those,
Every day every run, though tired ...
Cannot even utter the voice.

Life to be lived for the day is known,
Even then the piggy bank gets todays coin...
Future is an investment of the joy,
Only if today you enjoy.

Live each day with the moment it brings,
Sunshine, or the shed under the tree,
Nothing can make you as free,
The invaluable gifts that the nature has,
Everyday without a voice they teaches ...
Be hopeful even if some fool try to make you not so...
A joy ful face has more value than being a sorrow.

The Young Buds

Do not mess up with the growing soul,
Unmould as they are ...
There are better existence then yours in this nature,
To care and nurture.

Check the hands of your own,
Before you shake with them,
Look the path of your own before you, look them.
Tender blossom buds are they.

Allow the mind to comprehend,
Allow the brain to mature,
Do not try to hold the flow...
If you, are not so sure of your own glow.

Run Of A River

Ribbon of water, flowing down,
The dams, made of steel, before that even the sludge mad hardened,
Ever flowing gust of water as I flow,
Have anyone tried to stop me though.
I have a length and breadth of my own,
Bestowed by the mighty sky so unconquered,
The earth taking shape from molten lava, bear my weight,
I am called a river, a stream, creek or a brook.
Raising many a wonders of canyons and the falls...
I am running free ... I am running so wild !!!
What are you looking at me, my child ?
Run of a river at this stage is just the birth,

Face Of An Enemy

Trolling day in and day out,
So many of you I meet the diurnal ... un-account,
Whom to trust and whom to mistrust...
The enemy around have no faces to be seen.
Dark knighted man riding the black bronco.
The scarfed, and hooded, with an intended ride ...
They travel soft, soundless and highly booted.
Gusty night winds with heavy moist that captured,
More ways can be seen and felt to be lighter.
The house that is built around the canopies of wood,
So many merchants ready any time to woo !!!
The fish, in the calmness of water that was the safe home,
The soft sound of its flow, thus kept it engaged so ...
The octopus kept its look for it though,
Fragile fawn nested in the green blooms,
Roaring Lion kept the silence even,
Caught them amaze.
Dallies flying and sitting aloft on the garden of blossom,
The invisible web caught it for its hunger of the noon.

Tread, tread slow ...
Look as if you cross the road,
Fast traffic driven by so unknown ...
Who will hit whom is not known.

Landing At Home

Even if not travelled so far so long,
The thoughts of joy comes, even in thots,
Of landings make at home.

Calmness In Me And The Wholeness I Feel

Rested with you besides me,
I am rested for life now.
I am complete at last.
With the whole world surrendering to you,
Seized by the innocence and the silent moves.

The Fragrance, Of The Pervasive

Even after you left, the walls vibrate
The room is so full with your fragrant.
The unknown path of the allure...
Following like a revered soul.
Where do I get to see you,
Up, down and all besides me,
The emptiness has taken the spaces.
Like a mellowed voice I see,
From a distance of such cursed ...
Offering petals to the beloved lord,
Praying him to bridge the miles of sojourn.

Date For The Convict

In the walls of heart at solitude !
Rubbing back to back,
I stand counting on the dates,
You just pass them, my mate !!

The calenders hung in my home,
God knows who have even changed the year there on.
Who shall stand at the gate when I am left, or is it that I call someone.
Will there be someone standing by me then.

The times spent so alone, given me breadth that never was known,
Who steals and who do not,
Never could have brought out till I keep the loss.
Show me a man now my lord, who can be thus bestowed.
Who in this world will know the fervent desire of me for the date,
Next when I see a few delivering on my fate.

The Want Of The Poor

Never seen the rain of wealth so dreamt,
When would I loose the proverty enshrined !
I am waiting for a few penny to spend,
If at all I have them in my hands.

Look what I buy now and look what you did,
Spent a lot on luxury and I bought a silken gift,
The one that I shall pour on your feet of power,
Oh God, Please lift me from the daily fighting need of
the hour.

The Never Ending Pain Of Life

Even if you try, not so much vilify
The goodness in me remain, not to be so testified.
The joy or the feeling so called pain,
Is not in your dirty hands.
It is the rightness of some one much higher,
What you want to show me in despair.
The pain, the sorrow or the moment are now just in an alley so narrow...
I have broadened my life much with the verses of the past, so guiding me to my tomorrow.

The Nature Still Will Be Powerful

So many long bridges you have made,
So many colossal, walls...

Walking, running or driving each day,
I fail thus to find and obey,
The view that was far but so numb,
Uttering not a word it brought the unarmed calm.
Look not guide the closest of mine to further destroy,
The weakest seed and a plant without any voice,
For what I feel is they misconstrue the very fact,
Even if heavens fall, I shall still be the tall.

Answer From Where, Do You Expect ?

Going on a tour down below the place called earth,
Seen so many rivers melting into those paths,
They then flow into big- big oceans, sail the boat till then,
Is it beyond this is the heaven.

Each new born every-day, everywhere,
Are they replacing the one passed away...
Is the phenomenon of birth and death,
Is as, constant as the colossal mountains.

The nest built by the fragile flocks,
Could just blown away, by the tiniest of squalls.

The Rush On The Road

I have so much to offer ...
My beauty is in the simplicity !
Is truly gifted with no time in your hand,
Oh you the passer by, stop...
Stop a while to see the glimpses..
How much do you rush
How much do you drove me so fast
Take a time of breath for self.
Put a brake while you drive past
Hold for a moment of truth
Between the intersection of the roads...
Look beyond the windows of your roaring engines...
To realise it before you are lost.
Lost again, in the numerous calls and the mails that still unchecked ...unfinished
From even giving so much the day before, still vying for more.
All these people rushes away,
With a long distance and a point in mind far so far away !
In their minds everyday,
They forget I live here in this mid way.

I Am A Blessing Keep Me That Way !

Tiny tributaries of mine are bringing in lots of scrap...
I keep flowing in from here
I keep moving them with me
To the source of the life saver

One day few took time
They just felt choked by the splurge...
When I asked them the face
It's the same who travels ...
Long distances to see the shoreline

The debris are still far beneath not hidden much
They keep floating some might catch to be your own choking ...
I am a blessing flowing in side your towns
Not be polluted but to be felt.
For I can give enormous relief to soft wounded
I have the courage of silence with me
Even if my sharp fall ...it only brings

The Reasons To Be With You

No time is imperfect
When it comes to turning back
The waiting traffic does not matter
The door opening and garlanding you.

Why so much time was spent down
When final call was to meet you
In the process of selecting a few forgot to keep
my pressed gown.

Your observant eyes and your arms of strength
Have given me so much during the short
carnition ...
Love of the tiniest particle
And that of the mightiest creations
I felt sometimes so attached
Took some time that's why to detach.
Reasons to be with you are not there
Only the absolute truth to dare.
Bought dresses to wear each day
And forgot to keep the pressed gown.

Taken By Surprise

Remember the dearest one that you have lost
It;s a feeling of a stunner
That's so gone and true
Still dont you feel like deja vue.

If thats the moment of unacceptance
Accept them when time is in your hands
Don't sway them away
They may be the courage that you have.

You know when you go out of that cosy room of yours ...
Everybody stares you as if you are so not known
Recollect the few moments if you have good
Try to stitch them if you could.

Some one is eager to know what bites you
Some one is eager to see the news
Be the destined oneself to give them a

Call Of The Time

Done is the routine things
Just to keep saluting ...
Take me around and let me see
How pure form are thee...

Call of the time has come
To leap frog the dying lamb...
Muffle not the shout of desire
Let it flow like it wanted to throw...

Don't try to put off the fire
That has taken so much so time to attire
The channels of this river will
Take me through to the sea

Where a mighty new elements of almighty
Mixed up with the colour of you above thee
Shall give the courage of lost ones
When then we atleast realise
Standing by the vast shoreline
Bigger still bigger creatures exists
They are no one in this globe

They count very little in this world
How can they have so much dominance
You are the image of your own prominence
Run or crawl, it does not matter
What matters is the clarion call
Now is the time to put matters to recall
You have the legacy of the same God.
Take a discerning call of the time...
As they say ...it is the most interim
Also the most potent tool.
Rest assured as the time taken by you
Has made the harvest a golden pool
Plunge now if you think you are strong
Take the call, if you think you have the balls.

Building A Few Bridges

The mighty river was always so existed
Why now are you trying to make the bridges...
The connect of the north and south shore was always so present
Why are you trying to make it obvious...

The growth that you imminently want to show
Was always there that is how the river flow...
Farmers and the local lad made the fields to golden yield
There was no need to paste any to my mother's glow...
Look what you tried to do.
And peek now what is done
The bridges made and the outlooks are so distant
As if I agree now a days to none.
Receptivities are long lost ...
What is the use of these concocted

Means of coming nearer to some one
When the the self has so moved
It's tough now even that a hail of call
Does not make anyone to set a eye on
Let it rest in the Lap of wilderness
More meninngs that seem to be in them...
Rather than just trying so much to change.

A Burning Flower

There is a smell of variegated burn somewhere,
With the sunnyness everyone is up there,
Burgeoning buds looking for you...
The landing on it oh my bird !!!
Makes it unbroken and vivid,
With the day just spent with the familiar chores once again,
Where is the place to look for you in this heaven !
So that the era of my life left,
Be in your charming wings,
Busting and making me frothy,
The winds carry me where they go,
Make me sail and fly both.

At the mercy of human
A news spread that someone lost their puppy
3rd or 4th such, in a row,
Few days back a jungle fire
Caught by a few casual stroke ...
If you re so powerful a breed !
Don't leave anything at the mercy of the greed !
No control on the greed growing
It seems only a few flocks now remaining,
Branding the names of Good.
Pockets of desire mixed with impermanent affluence
by the wealth,
Not one but lot of things are at mercy of humans.

Even Death Is an Activity

The morning sun is up with such a bright light.
Passing through the routine of four phases.
The Twilight will offer it a graceful exit.
Even it is burning the hydrogen inside.
Swim like a duck and look at the moment.
The moment of love given by being existing.
Making each activity of the day as a part of the joy.
At the end there should be your bucket full of achieving times.
What count then will be the risks that you took...some faltered and some stood.
Sitting idle in the innumerable bubbles in the immense ocean...
Is it not inviting you to cast yourself.
Take time more and more
Not but that too long...
As the withering leaves of a deciduous tree
Loosing the beloved at the onset of a fall.
The rim in the crevasse for a climber
Is more narrower than the point of death.
Who in this globe is asking you to bed.

Tell them it's your own call that is Bieng redied now.
Shall have to wait to see what blooms now.
Enough of harshness that is showered from time to time.
It's a point now to gather few spread of dust...
Make it a paste of sandalwood
And carry on
Like a raging Bull with a showpiece Bi horn
What remains in his vein is the matter not known.
Rage on now and hence to make the others frighten ...
Not for the coz lesser than making your own self roar...
Roar ...roar for a success to be reborn.

The Butterflies and the Bees

Inspiration that you give
You are the maker of
The home of the beehive
One with a short few days
But see how high
See how wise I fly
One with soft humn
Has the power to build
The most sweetest of chyme
Flowers and my baby both wait for you ...
To come and charm us again and again.

Living and Learning Besides Brahmaputra

Brahmaputra
have seen him days in for long
He has enormous strength to carry on
He can take turns swiftly enough to save and run
He cuts smoothly those lands and changes direction
If time need be he saves smallest of creature by being a float even on the leaves
And have seen big burdened tree falling on him just like a helpless sheet
Sometimes even not visible to the boatman of his creed

Have taken lessons from him
So waiting for The day when

My call come
To tell them I have lived on those banks
And seen those saviour and recreants
This never ends
Being bold is not just a way I choose to be now
Rain or sunshine as the weather changes
The broad breadth of him has taught not to be threatened.

Motion of A Man

Sudden sheer of winds...light showers of rain
Does not make it even
When it comes to the breeze that your thots rein in
Nothing can be more stronger than a feeling
Of the heart smiling
That's coz you were and are part of the time
Of the motion of the man...most part of it
It were part woven with you.

It Still Remains

Looking At this peak which still remains
The energy in me never seems getting waste
The sky though not known in which shape
Shall embrace the moon above...
The next first sun rays will again evolve
Life after me still remains
A shallow wave of frightening
Made me feel things closer to me drifting away
Guided by the wise man's say
The infinite energy in me still remains
What is this feeling that I have today, neither happy
nor sad

Winning and even getting lost
Does not matter any more
The 4 directions has merged
And shown me something for the innerself to grow
Keeping the thots of the sages
In my mind
Always trying to make up my ever so lost time
Coming back to each breathe and inhaling them back

To make a hard stop realise
The fool in me still tries to be sad and worry
Come to me again and whisper in my ears
The you in me will always remain.

How Much More Pain

Pain pain and more pain
How much pain I need to gain
Or is it the life of me that you want
To be in around me
Is it that I be immobile or is it still more cry
What I do wrong cannot stop
Coz that I do not to remember you
It can only stop with you around me always
And nothing I can start and take it to finish without you.

The Tipping Point The End

Everything waits for the tipping point to arrive
The barren land ...
Look up to the mighty white sheet of sky ...
Waiting for the rain to arrive.
Revolving in the good and the bad days
The silence of the night..
Waits for the tiny so sweet
Chirps of the birds to arrive.
Each one of us holds each moment of life so worth...
Each one of us waits for the tipping point to arrive.

CPSIA information can be obtained
at www.ICGtesting.com
Printed in the USA
LVHW042130080222
710600LV00002B/65

9 781543 708448